SCRUMPTIOUS
PIES &
TARTS

SCRUMPTIOUS
PIES &
TARTS

LINDA COLLISTER
Photography by
Patrice de Villiers

RYLAND
PETERS
& SMALL

London New York

Art Director **Jacqui Small**

Art Editor **Penny Stock**

Editor **Elsa Petersen-Schepelern**

Photography **Patrice de Villiers**

Food Stylist **Linda Collister**

Stylist **Penny Markham**

Production **Kate Mackillop**

For Alan

Notes: Ovens should be preheated to the specified
temperatures—if using a fan-assisted oven, adjust time and
temperature according to the manufacturer's instructions.
Uncooked egg yolks should not be served to the very young, the
ill or elderly, or to pregnant women.

First published in the USA as *Basic Baking Pies and
Tarts* in 1997
This edition published in 2000 by
Ryland Peters & Small, Inc.,
150 West 56th Street, Suite 6303, New York, N.Y. 10019

10 9 8 7 6 5 4 3 2 1

Text © Linda Collister 1997
Design and photographs © Ryland Peters & Small 1997

Printed and bound in China by Toppan Printing Co.

ISBN 1-84172-101-8

A CIP catalog record for this book is available from
the Library of Congress.

CONTENTS

pies
and tarts

A tart or pie should be a successful combination of a **delicious filling** and a pastry that really does melt in your mouth.

Pastry is most easily made in a food processor, so don't worry if you have hot hands or a less-than-light touch. Just follow the rules; don't overwork or overstretch the pastry, or it will be tough and heavy, and don't allow the shortening to turn oily or start to melt as you work the dough, as this makes for soggy, greasy pastry. Use shortening straight from the fridge, chill the pastry before rolling out, then again before baking.

The pastry in most of these recipes is made in a food processor. However, to make pastry by hand, **sift** the dry ingredients into the mixing bowl. Add **very cold**, diced shortening, and toss until it is lightly coated in flour. Cut the shortening into smaller pieces using one or two round-bladed knives or a wire pastry cutter. **Gently** rub the shortening and flour between your **fingertips** (not your palms) a little at a time until the mixture looks like **fine crumbs** with no large lumps. As you work, lift your hands up to the rim of the bowl to aerate the mixture as it falls back into the bowl. Bind the mixture with ice water, egg yolk, or other liquid using just enough to make a soft dough.

If the dough is dry and hard it will be difficult to use, and if too wet and sticky it will be tough and heavy when baked. As soon as the dough comes together turn it out on to a lightly floured surface and **gently** and **briefly** knead the dough to make it smooth and even.

To line a tart pan, roll out the pastry on a lightly floured surface to the diameter of the pan plus twice its height. Roll the dough around the rolling pin and lift it over the pan. Gently unroll the dough so it drapes over the pan. **Carefully** press the dough on to the bottom of the pan and up the sides so there are no pockets of air. Roll the pin over the top of the pan to cut off the excess dough. The sides of the tart shell should stand slightly above the rim, in case it shrinks during baking, so use your thumbs to press the pastry sides upwards to make a neat rim about ¼ inch higher than the pan. **Curve** your forefinger inside this rim and gently press the pastry over your finger so it curves inwards, rather than overhanging the rim, to make unmolding easier.

The rim of the tart shell can be **fluted** gently with your fingers to match the fluting on the sides of the tart pan.

Baking blind (below center) produces a **crisp** tart shell. Prick the pastry with a fork, cut a round of non-stick parchment paper the same size as the pastry lining the pan, **crumple** the paper to make it flexible, open out, and gently press into the tart shell to cover the base and sides (easier if the pastry is chilled and firm). Press the paper into the angle where the sides meet the base. Fill the lined tart shell with ceramic baking beans, dried beans, or uncooked rice to weigh down. Bake in a preheated oven at 400°F for 15 minutes until lightly **golden** and just firm. Carefully remove the paper and beans then **lower** the temperature to 350°F. Bake for 5 to 7 minutes more until crisp and lightly golden.

To bake a filled tart, set it on a hot baking tray in the oven—the pastry will receive an **extra boost** of heat from the tray and this will prevent the filling making the pastry soggy.

lemon meringue pie

1 cup plus 2 tablespoons
all-purpose flour

a pinch of salt

1½ tablespoons superfine
or granulated sugar

1 stick (½ cup) sweet butter,
chilled and diced

1 large egg yolk, mixed
with 2 teaspoons ice water

Lemon Filling:

the juice and grated rind
of 3 medium unwaxed lemons

¼ cup cornstarch

1¼ cups water

2 large egg yolks

7 tablespoons superfine
or granulated sugar

½ stick (¼ cup) sweet
butter, diced

Meringue Topping:

3 large egg whites

¾ cup superfine or
granulated sugar

one 8¼-inch false-bottom tart pan

Serves 6–8

To make the pastry in a food processor put the flour, salt, sugar, and butter in the bowl and process until the mixture resembles fine crumbs.

With the machine running, add the egg yolk and water through the feed tube. Process just until the dough comes together. If there are dry crumbs in the bottom of the bowl, add a little more water, 1 teaspoon at a time, until you have a slightly firm dough.

To make the dough by hand, sift the flour, salt, and sugar into a mixing bowl then rub in the diced butter using the tips of your fingers. When the mixture resembles breadcrumbs, stir in the yolk and water mixture using a round-bladed knife—the mixture should be neither dry and crumbly nor soft and sticky. Wrap and chill for 15 minutes until firm.

Roll out the dough on a lightly floured surface to a circle about 10¼ inches across and use to line the tart pan. Prick the bottom of the pie shell all over with a fork then chill for about 15 minutes.

Bake the pie shell blind as described on page 9 in a preheated oven at 400°F for about 15 minutes until it is lightly golden and just firm.

Carefully remove the paper and beans, lower the oven temperature to 350°F, and bake for a further 5 to 7 minutes or until the base is crisp and lightly golden.

Remove from the oven and let cool while making the filling. Leave the oven at the same temperature.

Put the grated lemon rind and juice into a heatproof bowl. Add the cornstarch with about 1 to 2 tablespoons of the water. Stir to make a smooth paste.

Bring the rest of the water to a boil in a medium-sized pan, then stir into the lemon mixture. When thoroughly combined, tip the contents of the bowl back into the saucepan and cook, stirring constantly, until the mixture boils.

Reduce the heat and simmer, stirring frequently, for about 2 minutes until the mixture is smooth and thick.

Remove the pan from the heat and beat in the egg yolks and sugar followed by the butter.

Spoon the filling into the pie shell and spread it evenly.

To make the topping, put the 3 egg whites into a non-plastic, spotlessly clean, grease-free bowl and beat until soft peaks form. Beat in the sugar, 1 tablespoon at a time, then beat well to make a stiff, shiny meringue.

Gently spread the meringue over the lemon filling until completely covered.

Bake for 15 to 20 minutes in the preheated oven until the meringue is a good golden brown.

Let cool then unmold. Serve at room temperature within 24 hours of baking.

A traditional old-time *favorite* recipe, with a delicious lemon filling made rich and *creamy* with the addition of butter.

cherry almond pie

1⅔ cups all-purpose flour

a good pinch of salt

½ cup ground almonds

¾ cup plus 1 tablespoon
confectioners' sugar

1½ sticks (¾ cup) sweet butter,
chilled and diced

1 large egg yolk,
plus 1 teaspoon of ice water

Cherry Filling:

1 lb. large black cherries, stoned,
or frozen cherries*

2 tablespoons slivered almonds

2 teaspoons cornstarch

1–2 tablespoons light
brown sugar, or to taste

one 10¼-inch pie dish

one baking tray

Serves 6

*If using frozen cherries, use them
straight from the freezer. Sprinkle
the slivered almonds over the
pastry base and increase the
cornstarch to 1 tablespoon.*

Mix the flour, salt, almonds, and confectioners' sugar in a food processor. Add the butter and process until the mixture resembles fine crumbs. With the motor running, add the egg yolk and water through the tube until the mixture comes together. If there are dry crumbs and the dough does not come together, add ice water a little at a time. Wrap and chill for 15 minutes until firm enough to roll out.

To prepare the filling, put a slivered almond into the cavity of each cherry. Mix with the cornstarch and sugar.

Divide the dough in two, one part slightly smaller than the other. On a lightly floured surface, roll out the small piece to a circle 11½ inches across and use to line the pie dish, letting the excess drape over the rim. Spoon in the filling, leaving a border around the rim clear and mounding the fruit in the center. Brush the pastry rim with cold water. Roll out the remaining pastry to a 11½-inch circle. Roll it around the rolling pin, then unroll over the pie, draping it over the filling. To seal, press the top crust firmly onto the dampened rim then, using a small knife held vertically, cut around the edge of the crust to cut off the excess dough. Crimp the rim with the back of a fork or your fingertips. Make a steam hole in the center and decorate the top with pastry leaves.

Set the pie dish on a baking tray and cook in a preheated oven at 400°F for 20 minutes.

Reduce to 350°F, and bake for 10 minutes or until the pastry is golden. Sprinkle with sugar and serve warm or at room temperature. Eat within 24 hours of baking.

apricot crunch

1 cup all-purpose flour

¾ cup rolled oats

¾ cup light brown sugar

2 teaspoons ground cinnamon

1½ sticks (¾ cup) sweet butter,
chilled and diced

1 large egg, beaten

Apricot Filling:

1⅓ cups dried apricots

¾ cup unsweetened orange juice

a cinnamon stick

one 8¼-inch round pie dish,
about 1¾ inches deep

Serves 4–6

To make the filling, put the apricots, orange juice, and cinnamon stick into a non-aluminum saucepan and bring to a boil. Remove from the heat and let cool completely—preferably overnight. Drain thoroughly and discard the cinnamon stick.

To make the crust, mix the flour, oats, sugar, and cinnamon in a mixing bowl. Add the diced butter and rub in with your fingertips until the mixture resembles very coarse crumbs. Add the beaten egg and briefly mix into the crumbs with your fingers to make pea-sized lumps of dough—do not overmix or bind the dough together.

Set aside a third of the crust mixture. Scatter the remainder into the pie dish and press onto the base and up the sides using the back of a spoon or a fork. Spoon in the drained filling then lightly scatter over the reserved crust mixture. Bake in a preheated oven at 375°F for about 30 minutes until crisp and golden.

Serve warm or at room temperature with ice-cream or fromage frais. Eat within 24 hours of baking.

Dried **apricots,** *soaked in orange juice, make a delicious* **combination.**

Make this pie with your favorite berries. Mulberries were once rare, but are now **available** *in season in quality fruit shops and supermarkets.*

apple and berry
deep dish pie

In the bowl of a food processor, process the flour, salt, sugar, and butter until the mixture looks like fine crumbs. With the machine running, gradually add the water through the feed tube to make a soft but not sticky dough. Wrap and chill. Gently combine the apples with the berries and a little sugar to taste. If the apples are not juicy, add a tablespoon of water or lemon juice. Spoon the fruit into the pie dish, heaping it up well in the middle to support the pastry.

Turn the dough onto a lightly floured surface and roll it into an oval about 3 inches larger than your pie dish all the way around. Cut off a strip of dough about ½ inch wide, and long enough to go around the rim of the dish. Dampen the rim and paste on the strip of dough, joining the ends neatly. Dampen this pastry rim. Carefully cover the pie with the with the rest of the pastry, pressing it onto the rim to seal. With a sharp knife, trim the excess dough and use to decorate the top. Push up the sides of the crust with a small knife, then crimp or flute the pastry rim. Make a steam hole in the center, then bake the pie in a preheated oven at 400°F for about 30 minutes until the pastry is crisp and golden. Sprinkle with sugar and serve warm or at room temperature.

1 cup plus 3 tablespoons all-purpose flour

a good pinch of salt

1 teaspoon superfine or granulated sugar

¾ stick (6 tablespoons) sweet butter, chilled and diced

about 4 tablespoons ice water, to bind

Apple and Berry Filling:

about 2 lb. crisp tart apples, peeled, cored, and thickly sliced or diced

8 oz. raspberries, mulberries, loganberries, or blackberries

2 tablespoons superfine or granulated sugar, or to taste

one deep, oval pie dish, about 8½ inches long

Serves 6

fresh raspberry
lattice tart

1½ cups all-purpose flour

½ teaspoon baking powder

1½ oz. unblanched almonds

1 teaspoon ground cinnamon

½ cup superfine or
granulated sugar

1 stick (½ cup) sweet butter,
chilled and diced

1 egg, plus 1 yolk

Raspberry Filling:

8 oz. fresh raspberries*

1–2 teaspoons superfine or
granulated sugar, or to taste

1 rounded teaspoon cornstarch

sugar, for sprinkling

one 8¼ inch false-bottom tart pan

one baking tray

Serves 6

*Avoid washing the fruit if possible.
Pick it over well, checking for
blemishes and foreign objects.*

To make the pastry, put the flour, baking powder, almonds, cinnamon, and sugar into the bowl of a food processor and process until sandy-textured.

Add the pieces of chilled butter, and process again until the mixture resembles fine crumbs. With the machine running, add the egg and yolk, and process to make a soft dough. Wrap and chill the dough for at least 30 minutes until firm enough to roll out.

Turn out the dough onto a floured surface, and roll it out fairly thickly to a circle about 10 inches across. Use the pastry to line the tart pan, pressing the dough onto the base and sides. Trim off the excess pastry and use small pieces to repair any tears or holes, saving the remainder to make the strips of pastry lattice later. Chill the base and excess pastry.

To make the filling, mix the fresh raspberries with the sugar and cornstarch.

Re-roll the excess pastry, and cut it into wide strips.

Spoon the filling into the pastry-lined tart pan, and dampen the top edge with water.

Arrange the strips of pastry in a lattice on top, and press the ends onto the top edge to seal.

Set the tart pan on the baking tray, and cook in a preheated oven at 375°F until golden—about 25 minutes. Remove from the oven and sprinkle with sugar.

Serve the tart either warm, or at room temperature within 2 days of baking.

A fresh fruit **version** of Linzertorte, the classic tart from the town of Linz in Austria. The rich pastry is flavored and colored with **almonds** still in their brown papery skins, giving extra taste and **texture**.

Variations:

Strawberry Liqueur Lattice Tart

To vary the fresh fruit filling, omit the raspberries and sugar and substitute the same quantity of the finest quality strawberry jam or strawberry compote, mixed with about 2 tablespoons of schnapps or kirsch liqueur to taste. Proceed as in the main recipe. The alcohol will cut the sweetness of the jam filling.

Plum, Apricot, or Cherry Lattice Tart

For these three delicious variations, omit the raspberries and replace with a similar quantity of other fresh fruit. Choose from quartered, stoned fresh plums, halved and stoned fresh ripe apricots, or pitted fresh ripe red cherries. Sprinkle with 2 tablespoons of liqueur such as slivovitz (plum brandy) or kirsch and proceed as in the main recipe.

blueberry cheesecake tart

5½ oz. graham crackers, crushed

3 tablespoons sugar

5 tablespoons sweet butter, melted

Lemon Cheese Filling:

1 large unwaxed lemon

2⅔ cups cream cheese

1 teaspoon real vanilla essence

4 large eggs, beaten

¾ cup sugar

Blueberry Topping:

½ large unwaxed lemon

1¾ cups sour cream

½ teaspoon real vanilla extract

1 tablespoon sugar

8 oz. fresh or frozen blueberries

one 9-inch springform pan, greased

one baking tray

Serves 8–12

To make the crust, mix the cracker crumbs with the sugar and butter. Tip into the prepared pan and press onto the base and half-way up the sides, using the back of a spoon. Chill.

Grate the rind of the lemon. Put the cream cheese (at room temperature), vanilla, and lemon rind into the bowl of an electric mixer or processor and mix at low speed until the mixture is very smooth. Gradually beat in the eggs, increasing the speed as the mixture becomes softer. When thoroughly combined, beat in the sugar. Pour the filling into the crust and set the pan on a baking tray. Bake in a preheated oven at 350°F for 45 minutes. Remove from the oven and let cool a little—do not turn off the oven.

To make the topping, grate the lemon rind and thoroughly combine it with the sour cream, vanilla, and sugar, then gently spread over the top of the cheesecake. Top with the berries then bake for 10 minutes more.

Cool, chill overnight, then unmold. Remove from the fridge 30 minutes before serving. Store in a covered container in the fridge for up to 4 days.

A *combination* *of baked lemon cheesecake and blueberry pie—the **topping** is added toward the end of baking.*

To avoid a soggy pastry base, cook it thoroughly first, brush with egg white to seal, then cook the filled tart on a preheated baking tray.

lemon tart

1 cup all-purpose flour

a pinch of salt

¾ stick (6 tablespoons) sweet butter, chilled and diced

2 tablespoons sugar

1 large egg yolk

1–2 tablespoons ice water

a little egg white, lightly beaten, for brushing

Lemon Filling:

3 large eggs plus 1 yolk

⅔ cup double cream

½ cup sugar

the grated rind of 2 large unwaxed lemons

the juice of 3 large lemons

one 9-inch false-bottom tart pan

one baking tray

Serves 6

To make the pastry, put the flour, salt, butter, and sugar into a food processor and process until sandy-textured. With the machine running, add the egg yolk and water through the tube and process just until the dough comes together. Wrap and chill for about 30 minutes.

Roll out the dough on a lightly floured surface to a circle about 11 inches across. Use to line the tart pan, prick the bottom of the tart shell with a fork, then chill for 15 minutes. Bake the tart shell blind (see page 9) in a preheated oven at 375°F, then remove from the oven. Do not unmold but immediately brush the base with a little egg white then let cool. Reduce the oven temperature to 325°F and put a baking tray in the oven to heat.

To make the filling, put all the ingredients into a large pitcher and beat, by hand, until just combined. Set the tart shell, in the tart pan, on the hot baking tray and pour in three-quarters of the filling. Put into the oven then carefully pour in the remaining filling (this way you avoid spilling the filling as you put the tart into the oven).

Bake for 25 to 30 minutes or until the filling is firm when the tart is gently shaken. Let cool before unmolding.

Serve at room temperature or chilled.

sticky apple tart

To make the pastry, put the flour, salt, and butter into the bowl of a food processor. Process until the mixture resembles fine crumbs. With the machine running add 2 tablespoons ice water through the feed tube—the mixture should come together to make a firm dough. If the dough does not form a ball and is stiff and crumbly, add a little more water. In warm weather, or if the dough seems soft, wrap it and chill for about 20 minutes.

Roll out the dough on a lightly floured surface to a large circle, about 11 inches across, and use to line the pie dish. Press the pastry onto the base to eliminate any pockets of air, then trim off the excess with a sharp knife. The scraps can be saved for decorations. Decorate the rim of the tart by pressing the pastry with the prongs of a fork. Chill the tart shell while making the filling.

Peel, core, and coarsely grate the apple, then mix with the breadcrumbs, lemon rind and juice, and the golden syrup or corn syrup. Spoon into the tart shell—don't press down to level or compress the filling as you will lose its fluffy texture. You can decorate the tart with pastry scraps cut into leaves or apple shapes. Bake in a preheated oven at 375°F for about 30 minutes until golden. Serve warm or at room temperature within 48 hours of baking.

1½ cups all-purpose flour

a good pinch of salt

1⅓ sticks (¾ cup) sweet butter, chilled and diced

2–3 tablespoons ice water, to bind

Sticky Apple Filling:

1 large baking apple, such as winesap

3 rounded tablespoons golden syrup* or dark corn syrup

½ cup fresh white breadcrumbs

the grated rind and juice of 1 large unwaxed lemon

one 10¼-inch pie dish

Serves 6–8

Available in larger supermarkets and gourmet shops.

A classic English apple tart—best made with *baking* apples.

FRUIT **TARTS**

fig tart

10½ oz. ready-made puff pastry

Fig Topping:

12 ripe figs, rinsed

3 tablespoons Grand Marnier, Cointreau, or other orange liqueur

4 tablespoons apricot jelly or strained jam, to finish

Pastry Cream Filling:

1¼ cups whole milk

4 large egg yolks

4 tablespoons superfine or granulated sugar

2 tablespoons all-purpose flour

⅔ cup heavy cream, whipped

2 tablespoons orange liqueur, such as Grand Marnier

one 10-inch false-bottom tart pan

Serves 8

On a lightly floured surface, roll out the pastry to a circle 12½ inches across. Use the dough to line the tart pan, letting the excess drape over the rim.

Chill the pastry for about 15 minutes, then cut off the excess dough with a sharp knife.

Prick the base of the pastry with a fork, then line the tart shell with greaseproof paper, fill with baking beans, and bake blind (see page 9) in a preheated oven at 400°F for about 12 to 15 minutes until set.

Remove the beans and paper, then bake for about 10 minutes more until crisp and cooked through. Let cool while preparing the fruit and filling.

Trim the figs and cut them in half (or cut in quarters if very large). Sprinkle with the liqueur and leave to macerate for about 2 hours or overnight.

To make the pastry cream, first heat the milk almost to boiling point in a saucepan.

Put the yolks and sugar in a bowl and beat until light and thick, then beat in the flour. When the mixture is completely smooth, beat in the milk.

Tip the mixture back into the saucepan and cook, stirring constantly, until it boils and thickens. Simmer gently, still stirring, for 2 minutes, then remove from the heat. Sprinkle with a little sugar to prevent a skin forming, and let cool. When you are ready to serve, fold in the cream and liqueur into the pastry cream, and spoon it into the tart shell.

A summery, Mediterranean-style tart that makes a spectacular dinner-party dish.
Buttery, **crisp** puff pastry makes a base for ripe purple figs and pastry cream flavored with **orange** liqueur.

Drain the figs and reserve the liqueur. Arrange the fruit on top of the pastry cream filling. Heat the apricot jelly until smooth and very hot, then stir in the liqueur and quickly brush over the figs. Serve immediately.

Variation:

Prune and Pistachio Nut Tart

To make a prune tart, use the finest prunes. Remove the stones, then soak the fruit overnight in 3 tablespoons each of orange liqueur and orange juice. Make the tart shell and fill with pastry cream as in the main recipe. Thoroughly drain the prunes and arrange them on top. Heat 4 tablespoons redcurrant jelly, and brush over the fruit. Decorate with shelled, unsalted pistachio nuts blanched for a minute in boiling water to turn them bright green.

apple cinnamon tart

1 cup plus 3 tablespoons
all-purpose flour

a pinch of salt

1½ tablespoons sugar

1 stick (½ cup) sweet butter,
chilled and diced

1 egg yolk, mixed
with 3 teaspoons ice water

Apple Cinnamon Filling:

3 large cooking apples,
about 2 lb. total weight

2 teaspoons ground cinnamon

5 tablespoons sugar, or to taste

1½ oz. raisins, dried cherries,
or dried cranberries

2 tablespoons golden syrup*
or corn syrup

¼ stick (2 tablespoons) sweet
butter, chilled and diced

one deep, 9-inch tart pan

one baking tray

Serves 6

*Available in larger supermarkets
and gourmet shops.

To make the pastry, put the flour, salt, and sugar into the bowl of a food processor and process just until combined.

Add the butter and process until the mixture resembles fine crumbs. With the machine running, add the egg yolk and water through the tube and process just until the mixture comes together to make a slightly firm dough. If there are dry crumbs add a little extra water. Wrap and chill the dough for about 20 minutes.

Meanwhile preheat the oven to 400°F. Put a baking tray in the oven to heat up.

Roll out the pastry on a lightly floured surface to a large circle about 11½ inches across. Use to line the tart pan, and chill while preparing the filling.

Peel, quarter, and core the apples, then grate coarsely. Mix with the cinnamon, sugar, and dried fruit. Pile into the tart shell. Spoon over the golden syrup then dot with the pieces of butter. Set the tart pan on the hot baking tray and cook in the heated oven for about 20 minutes. Cool for a minute then unmold. Serve warm. Eat within 2 days of baking.

A good recipe to make with *windfall* apples, and a change from the usual sliced apple tarts.

caramelized pear tart

1⅓ cups all-purpose flour

a pinch of salt

¼ cup ground almonds

2½ tablespoons sugar

7 tablespoons sweet butter, chilled and diced

1 egg yolk

2–3 tablespoons ice water

Caramelized Pear Filling:

1 stick (½ cup) sweet butter

1 cup sugar

whole blanched almonds

about 4 lbs. William or Comice pears, slightly under-ripe, peeled and halved

one 12-inch tarte tatin pan, or skillet with an ovenproof handle

Serves 10

To make the pastry, put the flour, salt, ground almonds, and sugar into a food processor and combine briefly. Add the butter and process just until the mixture resembles breadcrumbs. With the machine running, add the egg yolk and 2 tablespoons ice water. Process just until the mixture binds to make a fairly firm dough (add extra water 1 teaspoon at a time if necessary). Wrap and chill for 20 minutes.

Slice the butter and arrange on the bottom of the pan or skillet to cover it completely. Sprinkle over an even layer of sugar, then almonds. Scoop the cores out of the pears with a teaspoon or the end of a vegetable peeler. Pack the pears into the pan, curved side up, then place over a moderate heat on top of the stove and cook for 20 minutes or until the butter and sugar have formed a richly golden caramel.

On a lightly floured surface, roll out the dough to a circle to fit the top of the pan. Roll up the dough around the rolling pin. Remove the pan from the heat and cool for 1 minute to allow the bubbling to subside. Lift the rolling pin over the pan and gently unroll the dough so it covers the filling. Quickly tuck the edges inside the pan. Prick the pastry with a fork, then bake in a preheated oven at 425°F for 20 minutes or until crisp and golden. Remove from the oven, leave for 5 minutes then run a round-bladed knife around the edge to loosen the pastry. Place a large plate upside down over the top of the pan and invert the tart so the fruit is uppermost. Serve warm or at room temperature within 24 hours of baking.

plum tart

To make the crust, first soften the butter. Put the flour, salt, and sugar into a mixing bowl, making a well in the center. Crumble the yeast into a small bowl with the milk, and stir until smooth. Pour the liquid into the well in the flour. Add the egg and butter, and gradually work in the flour to make a soft dough. Knead for 10 minutes until smooth and satiny—if the dough sticks to your fingers, work in extra flour a tablespoon at a time. The dough can be kneaded for 5 minutes using an electric mixer fitted with a dough hook, but do not use a food processor.

Cover and let rise for 1 hour at room temperature. To prepare the filling, toss the prepared plums with sugar to taste, and set aside.

To make the crumble topping, combine the flour with the sugar in a mixing bowl. Dice the butter and work it into the mixture with your fingers to make pea-sized clumps of dough. Stir in the nuts and set aside.

Punch down the risen dough with your knuckles, and roll or press it out to a rectangle about 12½ x 9½ inches. Transfer to the baking tray and press back to the correct size. Top with the plums, cut side up, then sprinkle with the topping. Bake in the preheated oven at 375°F for about 30 minutes until the base is golden, the fruit is tender, and the topping crisp and brown.

A German-style yeast-base tart.

1½ tablespoons sweet butter

about 2⅓ cups white bread flour

½ teaspoon salt

¼ cup sugar

½ cake compressed yeast

¾ cup milk, lukewarm

1 egg, beaten

Plum Filling:

1 lb. plums, halved and pitted

3 tablespoons raw or white sugar

Crumble Topping:

1 cup minus 1 tablespoon all-purpose flour

½ cup light brown sugar

1 stick (½ cup) sweet butter,

1⅓ cups walnut or pecan pieces

one large baking tray, greased

Serves 8

NUT TARTS AND PIES

hazelnut
strawberry tart

⅓ cup hazelnuts

1⅓ cups all-purpose flour

a pinch of salt

5½ tablespoons
confectioners' sugar

¾ cup (1½ sticks) sweet butter,
chilled and sliced

2 large egg yolks

Strawberry Topping:

1 lb. strawberries, raspberries,
blueberries, or a combination

⅔ cup seedless raspberry jelly

1–2 tablespoons water

one large baking tray, greased

Serves 8

Toast the hazelnuts in a preheated oven at 350°F until they are a good golden brown—about 8 minutes. If necessary, remove the papery brown husks by rubbing the nuts together in a clean tea towel. Let cool.

Save about a dozen nuts for decoration. Put the rest, with the flour and salt, into a food processor, and process them until sandy-textured. Add the confectioners' sugar and process briefly to combine. Add the diced butter and process until the mixture resembles breadcrumbs. With the machine running, add the yolks through the feed tube—process only until the mixture comes together. Shape into a ball and wrap. Chill until firm enough to roll out—about 30 minutes.

Roll or press out the pastry on the greased baking tray into a circle about 10¼ inches across. Flute the edges (decorate by pinching the pastry between your fingers). Prick the base all over with a fork, then chill until firm—10 to 15 minutes. Bake the tart shell for about 20 minutes or until firm and light gold (beware—overcooked pastry will taste bitter).

Leave until cool and quite firm, then transfer to a serving platter. Decorate the top with the reserved nuts and the strawberries—halved or quartered if large.

Heat the raspberry jelly with a tablespoon of water in a small pan, then beat until smooth. Bring to a boil, then brush over the fruit and nuts, completely covering them.

Leave to set, then serve with ice-cream or fruit.

A rich **hazelnut** cookie base is covered with small berries— strawberries, raspberries, even blueberries will do—then glazed. Simple but **glamorous.**

Variations:

Almond Strawberry Tart

Replace the hazelnuts with an equal quantity of blanched whole almonds. First toast the nuts in the oven until golden (take care not to let them burn), then cool. Save a few for decoration, then process the remainder with the flour and salt and proceed as in the main recipe.

Walnut Berry Tart

Omit the hazelnuts and substitute a similar quantity of walnut pieces—there is no need to toast them in the oven first. Proceed as in the main recipe.

Individual Strawberry Tarts

To make small, individual tarts to serve with tea or coffee, rather than as a dessert, cut the pastry into circles about 4 inches in diameter, using a cookie cutter or a small saucer to cut around. Proceed as in the main recipe, baking at the same temperature for about 10 to 12 minutes

pecan fudge pie

1 cup plus 2 tablespoons
all-purpose flour

a pinch of salt

¾ stick (6 tablespoons) sweet
butter, chilled and diced

2–3 tablespoons ice water.
to bind

Pecan Filling:

1 stick (½ cup) sweet
butter, melted

2 large eggs, beaten

¾ cup plus 2 tablespoons
light brown sugar

1 teaspoon real vanilla extract

¼ cup all-purpose flour

a good pinch of salt

⅓ cup unsweetened cocoa powder

1½ cups pecan halves

one 8½-inch false-bottom tart pan
or pie dish

Serves 8

To make the pastry, put the flour, salt, and butter into the bowl of a food processor and process until the mixture resembles fine crumbs. With the machine running, add 2 tablespoons of water through the tube and process just until the dough comes together. If there are dry crumbs in the bottom of the bowl and the dough seems stiff work in extra water, 1 teaspoon at a time, to make a fairly firm dough. In warm weather it may be necessary to wrap and chill the dough for 20 minutes before rolling out.

The dough can also be made by hand by rubbing the butter into the flour then stirring in enough water to bring the mixture together to make a fairly firm dough.

Turn out onto a lightly floured surface and roll out to a circle about 10¼ inches across. Use to line the tart pan, then chill. Let the butter cool to lukewarm.

In a mixing bowl lightly beat the eggs with the sugar and vanilla until frothy, then stir in the melted butter. Sift the flour with the salt and cocoa into the bowl then fold in with a large metal spoon. When thoroughly combined, mix in the pecans then spoon into the pie shell and bake in a preheated oven at 350°F for about 25 minutes until just firm. Let cool, then serve at room temperature. Eat within 3 days of baking.

*Really **fresh** pecans are essential for this recipe.*

sticky walnut tart

7 tablespoons sweet butter

1 cup plus 2 tablespoons
all-purpose flour

a good pinch of salt

1½ tablespoons sugar

1 egg yolk, mixed
with 2 teaspoons water

Walnut Filling:

1¾ cups walnut halves

¾ stick (6 tablespoons)
sweet butter

¼ cup sugar

2 oz. chilled honey

⅔ cup heavy cream

one 8½-inch false-bottom tart pan

Serves 8

To make the pastry, chill and dice the butter and place in the bowl of a food processor with the flour, salt, and sugar. Process until the mixture resembles fine crumbs. With the machine running add the yolk and water through the tube and process just until the mixture comes together. Chill until firm—about 20 minutes. Turn out onto a lightly floured surface and knead for a couple of seconds until smooth.

Roll out the dough to a circle 10½ inches across, then use to line the tart pan. Roll the dough around the rolling pin and lift it over the pan. Gently unroll the dough so it drapes over the pan. Carefully press the dough onto the bottom of the pan and up the sides so there are no air pockets. Roll the pin over the top of the pan to cut off the excess dough, then neaten the rim with your fingers. Chill for 15 minutes until firm.

Bake the tart shell blind, as described on page 9, in a preheated oven at 375°F. Remove the paper and beans and bake for another 5 minutes to cook the base—it should be firm and just colored.

Remove from the oven and let cool, but leave the oven on. Put the walnuts, butter, sugar, and honey into a heavy skillet, preferably non-stick. Cook, stirring, over low heat until the mixture is a pale straw gold. Stir in the cream and cook for 1 minute until bubbling.

Pour into the tart shell and bake for about 12 minutes until deep golden brown. Let cool, then unmold. Serve at room temperature with vanilla ice-cream or crème fraîche.

pignoli nut honey tart

To make the pastry, put the flour, salt, butter, and sugar into the bowl of a food processor. Process until the mixture resembles fine crumbs. With the motor running add the egg yolk and 1 tablespoon of water through the feed tube. Process until the dough just comes together. If there are dry crumbs or the dough is stiff, add extra water 1 teaspoon at a time to make a just-firm dough. Wrap and chill for 20 minutes.

On a lightly floured surface, roll out the dough to a large circle about 11 inches across. Use to line the tart pan, then chill while preparing the filling. Heat the oven to 375°F and put a baking tray into the oven to heat.

Beat the butter until creamy then beat in the sugar and honey. When fluffy, gradually beat in the eggs, 1 tablespoon at a time. Stir in the ground almonds, then sift the flour, salt, and baking powder into the bowl and mix gently. Spoon into the pie shell and smooth the surface. Set the tart pan on the hot baking tray and bake for 10 minutes. Gently remove from the oven and scatter the pignoli nuts on top of the filling. Bake for another 15 minutes until golden and just firm. Remove from the oven and let cool for 1 minute. Carefully unmold, let cool to room temperature, then serve.

Always use *fresh* nuts and store *opened* packets in the freezer.

1 cup all-purpose flour

a pinch of salt

¾ stick (6 tablespoons) sweet butter, chilled and diced

2½ tablespoons superfine or granulated sugar

1 large egg yolk

1–2 tablespoons ice water

Pignoli Nut Filling:

½ stick (¼ cup) sweet butter, at room temperature

6 tablespoons superfine or granulated sugar

1 tablespoon honey

2 eggs, beaten

⅔ cup ground almonds

2 tablespoons all-purpose flour

a pinch of salt

½ teaspoon baking powder

1 cup pignoli nuts

one 8½-inch false-bottom tart pan

Serves 6

pear and almond
cream pie

1⅔ cups all-purpose flour

a pinch of salt

1 stick (½ cup) plus 1 tablespoon
sweet butter, chilled and diced

3 tablespoons ice water, to bind

Pear and Almond Cream:

1 stick (½ cup) sweet butter,
at room temperature

8 oz. white marzipan
(almond paste), broken into
pea-sized pieces

2 tablespoons all-purpose flour

2 eggs, beaten

4 large slightly under-ripe pears,
peeled, quartered, and cored

sugar, for sprinkling

one deep, 10¼-inch
metal pie plate

Serves 8

Put the flour, salt, and butter into the bowl of a food processor and blend until the mixture looks like fine crumbs. With the machine running slowly, pour in the water through the tube—it should quickly come together to form a soft but not sticky dough. If there are crumbs work in extra water 1 teaspoon at a time. In hot weather wrap and chill until firm, then roll out.

Turn out onto a lightly floured surface. Cut off one-third to make the base. Wrap and chill the rest.

Roll out the base to a circle 12 inches across and use to line the pie plate, pressing the pastry onto the base and rim to push out any air bubbles. Do not trim off the excess.

To make the filling, process the butter and almond paste in a food processor until smooth. Add the flour and eggs and process until very smooth. Spoon onto the base. Cut the pear quarters into 2 to 3 vertical slices, ½ inch thick. Put on top of the almond mixture, so there is a slight mound in the middle. To make the lid, roll out the reserved pastry to a circle about 12½ inches across. Dampen the rim of the pie base then cover with the pastry lid. Press the edges together firmly to seal. With a sharp knife cut off the excess pastry and cut three slits in the pastry lid.

Bake in a preheated oven at 375°F for about 45 minutes, or until golden brown. Sprinkle with a little superfine sugar and let cool. Serve warm or at room temperature.

red fruit croustade

about 8 oz. phyllo pastry

about 1 stick (½ cup) sweet butter

Red Fruit Filling:

2 tablespoons sweet butter

1¼ cups fresh breadcrumbs

½ teaspoon ground cinnamon (optional)

3–4 tablespoons superfine or granulated sugar, to taste

1 lb. red fruit (blackberries, raspberries, cherries, red currants, black currants, or strawberries)

1 teaspoon cornstarch

confectioners' sugar, for sprinkling

one 12-inch springform pan, well greased and sprinkled with sugar

Serves 8

if necessary, thaw the pastry according to the package instructions. Once unwrapped, the pastry should be covered with plastic wrap or a damp cloth to keep it from drying out. If it becomes dry and hard, it will crack and become difficult to use. Meanwhile, melt the butter and let cool while preparing the filling.

To make the red fruit filling, first heat the butter in a small pan, then add the breadcrumbs and sauté until golden brown, stirring constantly.

Remove from the heat, and stir in the cinnamon and a tablespoon of sugar. Let cool.

Gently toss the prepared fruit with the cornstarch and the rest of the sugar.

Line the bottom of the prepared pan with 2 to 3 sheets of phyllo pastry, overlapping where necessary. Let the edges flop over the rim. Brush with melted butter, and sprinkle with a little superfine sugar. Add another 2 to 3 sheets of pastry, brushing and sprinkling as before. Repeat once more (about half the pastry should have been used).

Spread the breadcrumb mixture evenly in the pie shell. Add the filling, but do not press it down.

Fold the edges of the phyllo over the filling as if wrapping a package. Brush the top with butter and sprinkle with sugar. Lightly brush the remaining sheets of pastry with butter, then cut or tear them in half. Crumple each piece of pastry like a chiffon scarf, and gently arrange them in a pile on top of the

*Brands of phyllo pastry vary tremendously—I use Antoniou, which is **excellent**, others turn out tough and heavy. Ask other cooks for the best local product.*

pie. Sprinkle with any remaining sugar, and bake in a preheated oven at 425°F for about 15 to 20 minutes until golden. Carefully unclip the pan, dust with confectioners' sugar and serve.

Variations:

Caramelized Apple Croustade

Replace the red fruit with 2 lb. baking apples, peeled and thickly sliced. Heat 4 tablespoons butter in a skillet and sauté the apples until golden. Sprinkle with 5 tablespoons sugar and cook until the apples caramelize. Let cool, then proceed as in the main recipe.

Pineapple Croustade

Replace the red fruit with 1 medium-sized pineapple, peeled, cored, and cut into chunks. Heat 4 tablespoons butter in a skillet and sauté the pieces of pineapple until caramelized. Remove from the heat and stir in 2 tablespoons rum. Let cool, then proceed as in the main recipe.

mango tartes tatin

10½ oz. ready-made puff pastry

3 slightly under-ripe mangoes

2 pieces preserved stem ginger

¾ stick (6 tablespoons)
sweet butter

5½ tablespoons superfine or
granulated sugar

1 tablespoon shelled pistachio
nuts, blanched

two large baking trays

Serves 6

On a lightly floured surface, roll out the pastry as thinly as possible. Using a cookie cutter or a saucer as a guide, cut out 6 rounds 4½ inches across. Place on the baking trays, prick well, and chill while preparing the topping.

Peel the mangoes, and cut the flesh away from the stones. Cut the flesh into strips about ¾ inch thick. Chop the ginger very finely.

Heat the butter in a heavy skillet, then add the ginger. Roll the mango slices in sugar, then sauté in the hot butter until golden. Cool on a plate.

Arrange the mango slices on the pastry rounds, then bake for about 10 to 12 minutes in a preheated oven at 425°F until the pastry is golden.

Decorate with the pistachio nuts and serve immediately.

*Slices of mango are quickly **browned** in butter and sugar, flavored with **ginger**, and baked with puff pastry.*

crème brûlée tart

To make the pastry, process the flour, salt, and sugar in a food processor until just combined. Add the butter, and process until the mixture resembles fine crumbs. With the machine running, add the yolk and water through the tube, and process just until the dough comes together. Wrap and chill for 30 minutes. Turn the dough onto a lightly floured surface, roll it into a circle about 11½ inches across, and use to line the tart pan. Chill for 10 to 15 minutes.

Prick the pastry base, then cover with a circle of wax paper, fill it with baking beans, and bake blind (see page 9) in a preheated oven at 400°F for 10 minutes. Remove the beans and paper, and bake for 15 minutes more until the base is crisp and golden. Let cool, but do not unmold.

To make the filling, first arrange the fruit in the base of the cooked pie shell. In a heatproof bowl, beat the yolks and sugar with a beat until very thick and frothy.

Heat the cream and vanilla bean until steaming hot, but not boiling, then pour, beating constantly, onto the egg mixture in a slow, steady stream. Place the bowl over a pan of steaming water and cook slowly, stirring constantly, until thick—about 10 minutes. Remove the bowl from the heat, and remove the vanilla bean. Gradually beat in the butter, then pour the mixture into the pie shell. Let cool, then chill for several hours or overnight until firm and set. Sprinkle the sugar on top, then brown under a hot broiler for a few minutes. When cold, chill for 2 to 3 hours before serving.

1 cup plus 3 tablespoons all-purpose flour

a good pinch of salt

2½ tablespoons superfine or granulated sugar

¾ stick (6 tablespoons) sweet butter, chilled and diced

1 large egg yolk, plus 1 teaspoon water

Raspberry Filling:

4 oz. fresh raspberries

4 large egg yolks

5 tablespoons superfine or granulated sugar

1¾ cups heavy cream

1 vanilla bean, split

½ stick (¼ cup) sweet butter, diced, at room temperature

4 tablespoons sugar, for sprinkling

one deep, 9-inch false-bottom tart pan

Serves 8

torta di ricotta
with chocolate pieces

1 stick (½ cup) sweet butter

1 cup plus 1 tablespoon
all-purpose flour

3 tablespoons unsweetened cocoa

a pinch of salt

⅔ cup confectioners' sugar

Ricotta Filling:

3½ oz. unsweetened chocolate

8 oz. ricotta cheese

6½ tablespoons
confectioners' sugar

the grated rind of 1 orange

1 teaspoon orange liqueur
or real vanilla extract

1 large egg plus 1 yolk

⅓ cup flaked almonds, to finish

one 8½-inch false-bottom tart pan

Serves 8

To make the pastry, chill and dice the butter. Put the flour, cocoa, salt, and confectioners' sugar into a food processor and process briefly just to mix. Add the pieces of butter and process until sandy textured, then pulse the machine until the dough comes together. Wrap and chill for 20 minutes. Turn out onto a lightly floured surface and roll out to a circle about 10½ inches across and use to line the tart pan—the pastry is quite hard to work, so mend any holes that appear with trimmings, and press the dough together if necessary. Chill while preparing the filling.

To make the filling, coarsely chop the chocolate. Beat the ricotta until creamy using a wooden spoon. Beat in the confectioners' sugar followed by the orange rind and the liqueur. When completely blended, beat in the egg and the yolk, then stir in the pieces of chocolate. Spoon into the pie shell and sprinkle with the almonds.

Bake in a preheated oven at 350°F for about 25 minutes until firm. Let cool, then unmold. Serve at room temperature.

*The pie shell is made from a **rich** chocolate cookie mixture, and the light filling has ricotta studded with **chunks** of dark chocolate.*

torta di zabaglione

1½ cups whole blanched almonds

1 tablespoon confectioners' sugar

2 large egg whites

6 tablespoons superfine
or granulated sugar

1 teaspoon amaretto liqueur or
½ teaspoon pure almond extract

Zabaglione Filling:

4 large egg yolks*

3 tablespoons superfine
or granulated sugar

½ cup dry white wine or Marsala

⅔ cup chilled heavy cream,
whipped

fresh fruit, to decorate

one 9-inch springform pan,
greased and lined with non-stick
parchment paper

one large piping bag, fitted with
a ½-inch plain tube

Serves 6

*See note regarding raw eggs,
page 4.

Toast the almonds in a preheated oven at 350°F for about 10 to 12 minutes until light golden. Let cool. Reduce the oven temperature to 300°F.

To make the base, process the almonds and confectioners' sugar in a food processor until sandy-textured.

Put the egg whites into a spotlessly clean, grease-free, non-plastic bowl. Beat with a wire beater or electric mixer until stiff peaks form, then beat in the caster sugar, 1 tablespoon at a time. Using a large metal spoon, gently fold in the almond mixture and liqueur or almond extract. Spoon into the piping bag, and pipe a flat coil to cover the base of the prepared pan. Pipe a rim inside the edge of the pan. Bake the base for about 30 minutes until quite hard and golden brown. Cool, then unclip the pan and peel off the paper. Put the base on a platter and set aside.

To make the filling, put the yolks, sugar, and wine in a heatproof bowl set over a pan of boiling water. Beat until thick and foamy. Remove from the heat, and beat until cool. When completely cold, fold in the whipped cream, then spoon onto the crust. Decorate with fresh fruit and serve at once.

Marsala wine is traditionally used to make zabaglione, but if you find it too sweet in this dish, substitute dry white wine instead.